Fifty Days in

His

Pursuing Love

∽ D E V O T I O N A L ∽

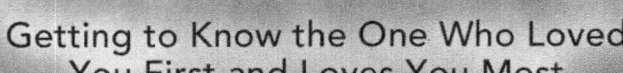

Getting to Know the One Who Loved
You First and Loves You Most

KIM K. FRANCIS

FIFTY DAYS IN HIS PURSUING LOVE DEVOTIONAL

Copyright © 2019 by Kim K. Francis

ISBN-13: 978-1-7329514-1-9

Kim K. Francis
622 S. Grinnell Street
Perryton, TX 79070
www.kimkfrancis.com
(806) 435-5575

To my son, Wes

ACKNOWLEDGMENT & INTRODUCTION

I want to thank my Spiritual Bridegroom, Jesus Christ, for wanting and loving me first and most! He wooed and pursued me until I fell head over heels in love with Him. He revealed the incredible wonders of His grace to my heart, and I marvel daily that I get to teach believers around the world how they can enjoy greater intimacy with Him through understanding their flawless identity in Him.

This fifty-day devotional is derived from the beautiful gospel truths presented in my first book, *His Banner over Me Is Pursuing Love: An Intimate, Interactive Study of the Song of Solomon, Chapters 1 and 2*. When you reach the end of *Fifty Days in His Pursuing Love Devotional: Getting to Know the One Who Loved You First and Loves You Most* and find yourself hungering for more of the same life-giving, liberating truths, I highly recommend that you immerse yourself in my in-depth study in order to experience greater intimacy with your Beloved. Get your digital or softcover copy at Amazon or a signed copy from www.kimkfrancis.com today!

CONTENTS

Day 1 – If Jesus Shared the Gospel

There are two kinds of people in this world: those who are in the spiritual realm of Adam and those who are in Me. The fullness of God lives inside My resurrected body. And those who are in Me, through My Spirit, are automatically in the Father. They are eternally and affectionately held within the Holy Trinity: God the Father, God the Son, and God the Spirit.

You may better understand this relationship by picturing a cube that represents the entire unseen spiritual world. Now see a Light-filled sphere floating in the center of the cube. This sphere represents My Spirit. Everything inside the sphere is spiritually alive, and everything outside the sphere is in the realm of Adam, in darkness, spiritually dead.

You are not a human body which contains a spirit. You are a spiritual being living inside a perishable human body. You communicate in this world through your soul (conscious awareness) and your body. And because of the fall of man—Adam and Eve's declaration of independence from Me in the garden of Eden—you were born into this world separated from My eternal life, in darkness, in the spiritual realm of Adam.

I created you. I knit you together in your mother's womb because I want you in My forever family. I love humanity so much that I willingly laid down My life to mend the separation between Me and them and to welcome all who will believe in (literally *into*) Me to My eternal family.

I am Unconditional Love personified. That's who I am. That's what I do. I can't help but love you with no strings attached, no matter what. I love you dearly and long for you to experience eternal life through believing into Me. But I have given you a free will and will not make this decision for you. If you pass from this earth separated from My eternal life—My Holy Spirit—then you will remain outside My family forevermore.

If, however, you believe that I died to mend our separation and have received the gift of My life, then you can *rest assured* that I have already taken you out of the spiritual kingdom of darkness (Adam) and immersed you into the spiritual kingdom of Light (Me).

You are now a beloved child of My Father because of your eternal spiritual union with Me, His only begotten Son. You are no longer dead in Adam but forever alive in Me. You are My flawless bride because of your eternal spiritual union with Me. Nothing you could ever think, say, or do will change this truth. Once you are in Me, you are in Me forevermore.

Inspired by Romans 5:12–21; 1 Corinthians 15:22; Colossians 2:9; John 14:20; 2 Corinthians 13:14; John 8:12; 12:46; Ephesians 2:1–5; Ezekiel 36:26; John 4:24; 2 Corinthians 5:1–6; 1 Thessalonians 5:23; Hebrews 4:12; Genesis 3; Psalm 139:13, 15; John 3:16; 1 John 4:9; John 3:18; Hebrews 9:27; John 14:6; Colossians 1:13; Galatians 3:26; John 1:12; Romans 8:16; 1 John 3:1; 1 Peter 3:18; John 3:29; 10:28; 2 Corinthians 11:2; Ephesians 5:22–32; Hebrews 13:5; Revelation 19:7–9; 21:2, 9; 22:17; 2 Timothy 2:13.

Day 2 – You Are Invited to Wondrous Delight in Christ

My flawless bride, I long for you to spend the time you have left on this earth fully believing that you are altogether beautiful, perfectly loved, highly valued, and completely accepted in Me. My heart's desire is that you live from your eternal spiritual union with Me in the same way that I lived while on this earth: entrusting Myself to and wholly dependent upon My Father.

Every day, I want you to fix your eyes on Me and your one and only flawless identity in Me. There is *not* a bad you and a good you. Believing this slanderous lie will undermine your experience of your righteousness, peace, and joy in Me.

As you focus on eternal spiritual truth, My 24/7/365 life within you will inspire and empower you from the *inside out*. I long for you to continually experience My cherishing love and exuberant life. When you let Me love you unconditionally and depend on My limitless power within you, you will automatically express Me in this world. I died *for* you so that I could live *in* you so that I could live *through* you in this world.

My greatest desire is for you to experience wondrous delight in intimacy with Me. Just as a husband and wife in the natural realm share a physical union and bear the fruit of children, you and I share a spiritual union where I have implanted you with My life and—with your cooperation—cause you to manifest the sweet, refreshing fruit of My Spirit: love, joy, peace, patience, kindness, goodness, faithfulness, gentleness, and self-control.

You are the love of My life, the object of My extravagant affection! When you begin to understand and habitually see yourself as My deeply cherished bride, you will begin to live like who you *already* are. Pure and simple, you will live loved and happy in Me, your Spiritual Bridegroom.

Inspired by Song of Songs 1:8, 15; 2:10, 13; 4:1, 7, 10; 5:9; 6:1, 4, 10; 7:1, 6; Jeremiah 31:3; John 3:16; 15:13; Romans 5:5, 8; 8:35–39; 1 John 3:1, 16; 4:8–10, 16, 18; Isaiah 43:4; Ephesians 1:4–6; Colossians 1:22; 1 Peter 2:23; John 5:30; 7:16; 8:28, 42; 12:49; 2 Corinthians 5:14; Hebrews 12:1–2; 2 Corinthians 5:17–21; Colossians 1:27; 3:1; Romans 14:17; 7:4; Galatians 5:22–23; Ephesians 5:9.

Day 3 – The Gift of Tranquility

Love of My life, My very Breath is the source of My written Word, the Holy Bible. I moved the pen of its every writer in order to reveal absolute truth—unchanging reality. My Word communicates how humanity can be reconciled to Me. It also teaches those who belong to Me how to walk in loving, trusting dependence on My 24/7/365 indwelling Spirit.

Nestled in the heart of My Word is My love song to you that I breathed into King Solomon about a thousand years before I became flesh and lived on this earth. The Song of Solomon is filled to the brim with poetic imagery, mirroring your eternal spiritual union with Me. *You are My heart's desire!*

The name *Solomon* is rich in meaning. It encompasses the calm serenity that accompanies covenant relationship with Me. The Jewish greeting, "Shalom," is found in this word. *Shalom* expresses well-wishes of peace, wholeness, and contentment to its recipient. Shortly after My resurrection, I greeted My disciples three times with the phrase "Peace be with you." This phrase communicates the eternal tranquil assurance every believer in Me can enjoy, regardless of their outward circumstances. This gift of tranquility is all-encompassing and has been completely paid for in advance through My finished work on the cross. Your belief in Me and acceptance of My life was all that was necessary for Me to complete you and give you peace with Me forevermore.

The covenant you and I share is a sacred covenant of marriage. I am your Spiritual Bridegroom and you are My flawless bride. This means that you are forever and completely at peace with Me because you are no longer separated from Me. Right here, right now, you are joined in eternal spiritual union with Me. You are altogether beautiful and possess all you will ever need for life and godliness. I am yours forever, and I will always be faithful to you, no matter what!

Inspired by 2 Timothy 3:16; John 17:17; Romans 5:10; 1 Peter 2:23; Galatians 5:16; Song of Songs 1:1; 7:10; John 20:19, 21, 26; 14:27; 19:30; 3:16; Colossians 2:10; Romans 5:1; 2 Corinthians 11:2; Revelation 19:7–9; John 10:28; 2 Timothy 2:13; Hebrews 13:5; Song of Songs 4:7; 2 Peter 1:3.

Day 4 – You Are Jesus' One and Only True Love

My deeply cherished bride, I long for you to personally experience My one-of-a-kind devotion for your heart alone. When you relate to Me, don't see yourself among the crowd of *God so loved the world*. See yourself as you truly are—standing alone in the heavenly spotlight of My affectionate gaze. I want you to realize through personal experience that *you* are My one and only true love.

Your brain may be going *tilt-tilt* right now, thinking that sounds arrogant and absurd. But aren't all things possible with Me? You have completely and utterly captured My heart forevermore. To see and experience yourself as My one and only true love will not puff you up. Instead, it will cause you to fall head over heels for the One who is already head over heels in love with you!

It is vital that you understand that My intimate love for you is not based on your behavior but on your union with Me in My crucifixion, burial, resurrection, and ascension. When you believed into Me, *the old you* in Adam was immersed into Me and was crucified with Me at Calvary. Then, you were buried with Me in the tomb, which proves the finality of the death of your old self in Me. Three days later, *the new you* was born again in My resurrection and is now and forever flawlessly fused to My Holy Spirit. There is therefore now no such thing as you apart from Me! You are one spirit with Me, and all of My attributes (except Deity)—which include My *faith*—belong to you.

Don't ever again fall for the lie that you don't have enough faith. Your new identity in Me is equipped with the faith that I perfectly exercised in My Father while I walked this earth. In this moment and the next, you can choose to walk by My faith and enjoy My exclusive love for you.

Inspired by Song of Songs 2:7; 3:5; 7:6; 8:4; Jeremiah 31:3; John 3:16; 15:13; Romans 5:5, 8; 8:38–39; 2 Corinthians 5:14; Ephesians 1:4–5; 2:4–6; 3:16–21; Mark 10:27; Romans 6:6–7; Galatians 2:20; Colossians 1:22; 2:12–13; 3:1–4; 1 Peter 1:3; 2:24; 1 Corinthians 1:30; 3:16; 6:17; 2 Corinthians 5:7, 17, 21; Galatians 5:16, 25.

Day 5 – Your Indestructible Union with Christ

My one and only true love, no one can kiss two people at the same time. A kiss is an expression of an intimate relationship. Our Divine romance started with the kiss of your salvation, your deliverance out of the spiritual realm of Adam into Me, your Spiritual Bridegroom.

My Spirit first awakened you to My love for you by grace—My unprovoked favor and tender loving-kindness toward you. And through your initial belief into Me, you became Mine forevermore. My eternal life is a matchless gift from Me to you, My beloved bride. You could never earn Me nor deserve Me, but only willingly receive Me into your heart. And this reception happens only one time. In the same moment you believed into Me, My Spirit moved into your new spirit. Our eternal spiritual union is your new heart. *I in you and you in Me for all eternity.*

We will never divorce because I will never leave you nor forsake you, regardless of what you may or may not do. Our eternal spiritual union is unbreakable, unshakeable, and indestructible. Even if you are deceived into believing that you can walk away from Me, it is simply not possible. I am with you always and forevermore.

Inspired by Colossians 1:13; Ephesians 2:8–9; Song of Songs 2:16; 6:3; 7:10; John 4:10; Acts 8:20; Romans 5:15; 6:23; John 3:16; Ezekiel 36:26; John 14:20; 15:4; 17:21; Hebrews 13:5; John 10:28; 2 Timothy 2:13; Matthew 28:20; Romans 8:38–39.

Day 6 – You Are Forgiven for the Sins of Your Lifetime

My forever love, you may be surprised to learn that your salvation has three extraordinary facets to it. When you believed into Me, you received a triple-crown kiss, secured through your union with Me in My death, burial, resurrection, and ascension. This kiss encompasses complete forgiveness of sins, an irreversible identity change, and an eternal life change.

You may find this difficult to believe, but *you have been completely forgiven for the sins of your entire lifetime*. It's true! When you were dead in your transgressions, My Father made you alive together with Me, having forgiven you all your sins. He canceled your lifetime sin debt (including your future sins), nailing it to the cross. If you believe that I forgave all of your sins up until the moment you accepted Me, but then after that, you have to ask forgiveness for every sin you commit, then what will happen if you forget one?

Imagine that your wealthy earthly husband never wants you to do without anything you need or want. So, he deposits a massive sum of money into a savings account to cover every debt you will incur throughout your lifetime. But there's a catch. Your checking account has a zero balance. Every time you write a check, you have to tell him what you bought and how much it cost. Then, you have to ask him to transfer the exact amount from the savings account to cover your transaction so that you won't overdraw your checking account. While you would be extremely thankful your generous husband always agrees to pay each debt, the consequences (overdraft fees, embarrassment) will be costly if you forget even one.

If you are anxious about the possibility that some of your sins have not been forgiven because you can't remember them all, then *rest easy.* I deposited My unlimited riches into your checking account instead! You never have to worry about incurring hefty insufficient funds fees for unconfessed debts.

Will this knowledge make you any less appreciative of My overwhelming generosity? Of course not! It will make you even more thankful that you can lay your head on your pillow every night and sleep in sweet peace, knowing that you will never have to work to pay off your sin debt. I really did pay it *all* with the first and only forgiveness deposit the moment you and I were joined together in sacred union.

Inspired by John 3:16; Romans 6:3–7; Galatians 2:20; Colossians 1:22; 2:12–14; 3:1–4; 1 Peter 1:3; 2:24; Ephesians 1:7; 4:32; Colossians 1:13–14; John 1:29; Hebrews 9:22, 26, 28; 10:1–3, 10–14, 18; 1 Peter 3:18; 1 John 3:5.

Day 7 – You Can Sin All You Want?

My spotless bride, if you believe that I forgave all the sins of your past the moment you believed into Me, but from then on you have to remember and ask My forgiveness for each one, your focus will be shifted away from what *I have already accomplished for you* to what you must do to remain in "good standing" with Me. The best news ever is that I forgave the sins of your entire lifetime the moment you first believed.

Christians who believe that lifetime forgiveness of sins is just too good to be true will often highlight *one* verse from the first letter that My apostle John wrote as the basis for their belief. They use this verse outside of its context to try and prove that believers have to keep asking Me for forgiveness in order to stay clean: "If we confess our sins, He is faithful and righteous to forgive us our sins and to cleanse us from all unrighteousness." A conundrum, however, is presented just thirteen verses later: "I am writing to you, little children, because your sins have been forgiven you for His name's sake."

These two verses cannot possibly be true at the same time—unless they are addressed to two different audiences. In the first verse, John was appealing to Gnostics to believe in Me and be saved. Gnostics were those who had infiltrated the early church and believed that they had no sin. In contrast, the second verse is unmistakably addressing believers—"little children" whose sins have *already* been forgiven for My name's sake.

Those who teach that believers have been forgiven for the sins of their lifetime often get accused of giving Christians a green light to sin. This is almost laughable to Me—as if sinning is what those who are joined to Me really *want* to do. Inherent in the believer's new "heart-ware" are desires that perfectly match Mine.

When you fully understand that you have been made clean forever, regardless of what you do or don't do, you will celebrate the liberating realization that *you really don't want to sin*. Your new heart's desire is to express My cherishing love, exuberant joy, perfect peace, enduring patience, overflowing kindness, all-encompassing goodness, unwavering faithfulness, compassionate gentleness, and self-control at all times.

Inspired by 1 John 1:9; 2:12; Romans 6:1–2, 21; Jeremiah 31:31–34; Philippians 2:13; Hebrews 8:10–12; 10:10, 14, 16–18; Ezekiel 11:19; 36:25–27; Galatians 5:16–17, 22–24.

Day 8 – Healthy New-Life-in-Christ Habits

My holy bride, confession and repentance are healthy habits that will benefit you when you realize your thoughts, feelings, and actions aren't an expression of your new heart in Me. *Confession* simply means to agree with Me that the ways in which you are thinking, feeling, and acting aren't in harmony with My Spirit. This usually happens when you take your focus off of our holy union and your peace and joy diminish.

Repentance simply means to stop paying attention to the disturbing circumstances surrounding you and the distressing noise in your head and start focusing on what is true in your new heart—Me and you, together forever. Vibrant new life is expressed through your thoughts, feelings, and actions when you exercise trusting dependence on My powerful Presence within you.

When you realize you are acting like someone you're not, it makes perfect sense for you to experience godly sorrow that leads to repentance. Telling Me you are sorry for not walking in the truth of your new identity by the power of My Spirit and thanking Me for the forgiveness that is *already* yours delights My heart! Nevertheless, your confession and repentance do not make you any cleaner or closer to Me. My shed blood and your initial belief into Me secured an eternally clean heart for you through our holy union.

In light of your knowledge of your eternal cleanliness and closeness to Me, it is, however, important for you to realize that your complete forgiveness before Me will not shield you from the earthly consequences of your sin. It also doesn't mean that you don't seek forgiveness from other people when you sin against them. In order to maintain healthy relationships, admit your wrongdoing and seek forgiveness from the person you have injured. And be quick to forgive others by the power of My indwelling Spirit when they sin against you.

I want you to wake up every morning believing that you stand completely forgiven in Me. This may not be something you fully understand with your mind or feel with your emotions, but you can choose with your will to believe it, regardless of opposing thoughts or feelings. With practice, you will find it easier to believe your way into a new way of feeling than to try to feel your way into a new way of believing.

Inspired by 1 Corinthians 3:17; Hebrews 3:1; 4:14; 10:23; Ezekiel 36:26; 2 Corinthians 5:17; Galatians 5:16, 25; Romans 8:6; 2 Corinthians 7:9–11; Ephesians 1:7; 4:32; Colossians 1:13–14; 2:13–14; Hebrews 9:22; Colossians 3:12–13; Luke 23:34; 2 Corinthians 5:7; Galatians 2:20.

Day 9 – The Marvelous Truth

My forever love, there is absolutely nothing you could think, say, or do that could separate you from Me and My love for you. New covenant grace is the ruling order of every moment of your new life in Me. I entered into a sacred marriage covenant with you when you literally believed yourself right into Me!

This covenant is not a mere contract. A contract is a legally binding written agreement between two parties who agree to do their parts. It becomes null and void when either party fails to keep up his or her end of the agreement. You can think of a contract like a handshake. When one person lets go, the agreement is broken.

While a covenant is also a legally binding written agreement, it holds much more weight than a contract. It cannot be broken unless both parties fail to do their parts. The Roman handshake is a wonderful visual of covenant. Each person grasps the wrist of the other person. If one person lets go, the agreement is still binding because the other party continues holding on to the wrist of the one who let go. Both parties have to let go in order for a covenant to become null and void.

The marvelous truth is that *I will never let go of you*, desert you, forsake you, or stop being faithful to you—regardless of what you may think or feel or do. Because of our eternal spiritual union, it is impossible for Me to disown you. The reason should be crystal clear: I cannot disown Myself!

This knowledge of your covenant relationship with Me is further assurance of your eternal security in Me. No earthly marriage could ever compare to our eternal spiritual union. You are My gorgeous bride and I am Faithful and True—your forever Spiritual Bridegroom!

Inspired by Romans 8:38–39; Jeremiah 31:31–34; Luke 22:20; 1 Corinthians 11:25; 2 Corinthians 3:6; Hebrews 8:8–13; 9:15; 12:24; John 10:28; Hebrews 13:5; 2 Timothy 2:13; Revelation 19:7–9, 11.

Day 10 – Your Sweet Rest in Mr. Grace

My endless love, My Spirit is the Spirit of grace. Simply put, I am Grace personified. And there is nothing kinder, nothing more loving that I could do for you than to make eternal union with My Holy Spirit possible.

For the unbeliever, grace is My eternal life available for the asking; it's a gift to be received through believing into Me. And this gift was made possible when I laid down My life on the cross. For you, My beloved bride, grace is the 24/7/365 availability of My life to be enjoyed by you and expressed through you. When you believed into Me, you received the fullness of My grace. And *fullness* means "fullness."

When you believe, either consciously or subconsciously, that you are lacking anything you need from Me or that you have to earn or deserve what you receive from Me, you are erroneously living under a law-based system rather than grace. That's like a royal choosing to live as a homeless person on the streets.

The Law was given as a standard for living—a way to define sin—and to ultimately cause all who are living under it to throw up their hands in utter frustration because they could not keep it perfectly. Perfection is the Law's standard, and no one except Me lived a perfect, sinless life.

My apostle Paul communicated My purpose for the Law beautifully when he told the church at Galatia that it is the guardian that takes you by the hand to lead you to Me so that you can be made right with Me through faith. Your life of faith in Me and My finished work on your behalf is intended to be one of sweet rest. A privileged life where you simply trust My indwelling Spirit to inspire and empower your living from the inside out.

Inspired by Hebrews 10:29; John 1:14; 3:16; 1:16; Romans 6:14–15; Matthew 5:48; Galatians 3:10; James 2:10; Romans 2:14; 4:13; Galatians 3:29, 24; John 19:30; Hebrews 4:1, 3, 8–11.

Day 11 – You Are Righteous and Holy through Faith

My beloved, even though the Law wasn't given directly to Gentiles, every person who tries to achieve righteousness through what they do or don't do is still living under their own self-imposed law-based system.

This might lead you to wonder if the Law is bad. It isn't. I did not come to do away with the Law, but to fulfill it. *On a bloody cross.* I lived a sinless life, making it possible for everyone who believes into Me to become the "righteousness of God." Take time to let that sink in. I put an end to your futile attempts to *earn* righteousness and imparted My very own righteousness as a *gift* to you the moment you believed into Me.

Sadly, many who belong to Me are still living under a law-based system simply because *they do not know who they already are.* Born into a world saturated with performance-based standards, they still believe they have to do something for Me in order to stay in "right" relationship with Me and earn My affection. This belief and the behavior that follows completely disregard My finished work. Law causes a believer to focus on their performance *for* Me; grace causes a believer to focus on My perfect performance on their behalf and motivates them to live *from* My abundant life within.

If you fail to understand grace, you will inevitably experience unnecessary bondage to a performance-based lifestyle, trying to earn or deserve My blessings and favor. This is as ridiculous as trying to walk into a room you are already in. It's impossible because you are already there! You have already been blessed with every spiritual blessing in Me. *Can you believe that?* You no longer have to ask for spiritual blessings because you already have My Spirit living in you without interruption!

What's more, *you* are where I live, and any place I live is *anointed*—permeated with My holiness. You are not holy because you act holy. You are already and forever holy through your eternal spiritual union with Me.

As you set your mind on the truth of your eternally righteous and holy identity, righteousness and holiness will naturally exude through your life.

Inspired by Leviticus 26:46; Psalm 147:19–20; Matthew 5:17; John 3:16; 2 Corinthians 5:21; Romans 3:21–24; 5:17; John 19:30; 1:14, 16–17; Ephesians 1:3; 1 Corinthians 1:21; 1 John 2:20, 27; Romans 11:16; 1 Corinthians 3:17; Ephesians 1:4; 5:27; Colossians 1:22; 3:12; Revelation 21:2, 10; 22:11; 1 Peter 1:15–16; 2 Peter 3:11.

Day 12 – You Are Forever Alive and Flawless in Christ

My holy bride, you may be thinking there has to be more than what you are currently experiencing in your relationship with Me. The answer to enjoying greater intimacy with Me in the here and now lies largely in your understanding the fullness of the triple-crown kiss of salvation you received when you first believed into Me.

While your *lifetime forgiveness* is absolutely wonderful, the remaining two aspects of your triple-crown kiss are equally as marvelous: your *irreversible identity change* and *complete life change*. When you begin to feast your eyes on your one and only flawless identity in Me, you will be open to experiencing wondrous delight in intimacy with Me. Just think about it. If you see yourself as a dirty rotten sinner, chances are you won't be too excited about asking a holy God to cause you to experience His affection.

My heart is who I am, and I am Spirit. You too are a spiritual being—a spiritual heart. Experiential intimacy with Me would be impossible if not for our spiritual "heart" union that began at salvation. Every person born into this world is a spiritual heart separated from My life (Spirit) because of the fall of man in the garden of Eden. Your entrance into this world was a spiritual stillbirth; you were born separated from My eternal life.

Simply put, *spiritual death* describes the separation of man and God, and *spiritual life* is the union of man and God. I came to earth to mend the spiritual separation between God and man. And those who believe into Me have already been transferred out of death into My eternal life. My dear bride, how I long for you to rest and rejoice in the truth that you are already and forever alive and flawless because of your eternal heart union with Me.

Inspired by Song of Songs 2:14; 4:7; 2 Corinthians 5:17, 21; John 14:16–17; 1 Corinthians 6:17; John 4:24; Ezekiel 36:26; 1 Thessalonians 5:23; Hebrews 4:12; Genesis 2:17; 1 Corinthians 15:22; John 3:36; 5:25; 6:47; 11:25.

Day 13 – Who Do You Believe You Are?

My dearest darling, your spiritual heart is the essence of your being; it is who you are at the core. Your soul is where you experience conscious thoughts, feelings, attitudes, desires, and choices. These in turn influence your actions. Your body is your physical house—where you experience this tangible world through your five senses of sight, hearing, touch, taste, and smell, and express action. Simply put, your spiritual heart is *who you are* and your soul and body are *where you do who you are*.

My greatest desire is that every person's desperately sick and deceitful heart be replaced with a new spiritual heart through their belief into Me. And once a person receives their new spiritual heart—their new spirit united with My Holy Spirit—all I want is one thing: for them to rely on My 24/7/365 indwelling Spirit to inspire and empower their new-heart living from the inside out.

The most wonderful news of all is that your new spiritual heart in Me is saturated with desires that perfectly match My heart's desires. You no longer *want* to sin. Instead, you desire to glorify Me in all that you think, feel, say, and do. Isn't this absolutely liberating to realize?

Because the spiritual realm is unseen and unfelt with the physical senses, the degree to which you will live out your true identity (your new spiritual heart) will be the degree to which you live out *who you believe you are* rather than simply who you are.

So the most important question for you, My beloved, is "Who do you believe you are?" Your answer will determine whether you glorify Me by walking by My Spirit or quench My Spirit by walking according to the flesh. Your answer will determine whether you live your days in wondrous delight in intimacy with Me or with senseless spiritual amnesia.

Ask my Spirit to illumine your mind with these phenomenal truths about who you *already* are. You will be amazed (and grateful) as you daily witness the progressive expression of your true identity in Me!

Inspired by Ezekiel 36:25–27; 1 Thessalonians 5:23; Hebrews 4:12; 2 Corinthians 5:1–4; Jeremiah 17:9; 2 Corinthians 5:17, 21; John 3:16; 1 Corinthians 3:16–17; 6:17; Romans 15:18; Philippians 2:13; Jeremiah 31:31–34;

Hebrews 8:10–12; 1 Corinthians 6:20; 2 Corinthians 5:7; Galatians 5:16, 25; 1 Thessalonians 5:19; 2 Corinthians 3:16–18.

Day 14 – No Shoulds, Oughts, or Musts Allowed!

My beautiful love, I am your very Life source. When I am revealed to the world at the end of the age, you too will be revealed with Me in glory. This is because there is now no such thing as "you apart from Me."

Everything I inspire you to do, I empower you to do. Rest in knowing I've got your back in everything, regardless of what it may look like in the natural realm. This includes your mistakes, missteps, and flesh trips.

My unchanging love for you has been poured out within your heart through My Spirit who was given to you when you first believed. I work in you continually, motivating you to express my delightful intentions.

Think about it this way: you have My very thoughts within you waiting to be uploaded by faith to your conscious awareness.

While it is true that sometimes the thoughts you experience are the result of My spontaneous inspiration, I want you to realize that you have the incredible privilege of continually choosing to renew your thinking to reflect your brand-new identity in Me.

You now share in My authentic traits of love, joy, peace, patience, kindness, goodness, faithfulness, gentleness, and self-control because we are one spirit together in holy matrimony. When you allow yourself to savor My love, joy, peace, patience, kindness, goodness, faithfulness, gentleness, and power toward you, these characteristics will automatically be expressed in your daily living. *Ahhh!* I long for you to experience the restful, refreshing life inspired by My gently flowing grace. A life in which no *shoulds*, *oughts*, or *musts* exist. A life motivated by your new heart's holy desires.

All of these qualities are given to you by grace through faith—not as a result of works. If you could muster them up, they would be called "works," not fruit. I've simply called you to believe and rest in My finished work on the cross on your behalf. When you do that, you will be amazed at the gorgeousness being expressed through your Monday-through-Sunday living!

Inspired by Song of Songs 4:7; Colossians 3:4; 1 Corinthians 6:17; Philippians 2:13; 4:13; Romans 8:31; 5:5; 8:9–11; 1 Corinthians 2:16; Romans 12:1–2; 2

Corinthians 5:17; Galatians 5:22–23; Ephesians 5:22–32; Matthew 11:28–30; Jeremiah 31:33; Hebrews 8:10; Ephesians 2:8–9; John 6:28–29; Hebrews 4:3; John 19:30; Colossians 3:12–14.

Day 15 – He's Singing and Dancing over You with Joy

My glorious one, whether you are a new believer or you have been in Me for years, it is vital that you understand you aren't necessarily going to *feel* like a brand-new person 24/7/365. Feelings are in the realm of the soul and body, both of which are subject to the influences of the world in which you live.

Your new birth is in your spiritual heart and involves faith—believing in the unseen or the unfelt. Even though you may not see or feel the truth that your identity has changed, you can *know* it through believing My Word. Bottom line: your new birth is an eternal spiritual reality.

Because I have brought you into eternal spiritual union with Me, you can ask Me to cause you to experience greater intimacy with Me. This comes from fastening your attention on My indwelling Spirit in your heart, talking to Me, and listening for My response to you.

The marvelous truth is that I am in you and I continually sing and dance over you with joy! Why? Because you said *yes* to My invitation to enter into this Divine romance! You can rest assured that your sins are gone and you are complete in Me. I am fully satisfied with who you are now and forevermore.

Inspired by John 17:22; 2 Corinthians 5:17; 1 Thessalonians 5:23; Hebrews 4:12; John 3:3; Hebrews 11:1; John 8:32; 1 John 2:21; 1 Corinthians 6:17; John 16:24; Matthew 21:22; Isaiah 26:3; Colossians 3:1–4; Hebrews 12:1–2; Colossians 1:27; Zephaniah 3:17; 1 John 3:5; Colossians 2:10.

Day 16 – Love Notes from Your Beloved

My dearest darling, *you* are the object of My extravagant affection. While it is true that—in this world—you won't feel My special love for you every second of every day, there are things you can do to facilitate your enjoyment of delightful intimacy with Me. If you want to spend time with loved ones amidst life's distractions and jam-packed schedules, you have to be intentional. It's the same with our Divine romance.

A good place to start when you are spending focused time with Me is My written Word. Interspersed throughout its pages are Love Notes straight from My heart to yours. Even though you and I are joined together in spirit right now (and forever), you do not yet see Me in My resurrected body. In your mind's eye, picture Me sitting at a desk with a blank sheet of paper and a pen in hand. As I gaze at your portrait, I can't help but smile because *you said yes* to eternal union with Me. My one-of-a-kind love for *you* swells within my heart and overflows as I begin to write intimate Love Notes to you.

There has never been a moment when I have not deeply cherished and adored you. I love you so much, that I paid the ultimate price for you so that we could be united forever in holy spiritual union. When you said yes to eternal union with Me, My heart was filled with ecstatic joy! Your yes alone made the cross worthwhile.

Through My indwelling Spirit, I have saturated your heart with My special love for you. My love for you is perfect and will drive every fear out of your life when you meditate on it. It is impossible for you to enjoy My love and be afraid at the same time. You can rest assured that I'm going to keep on loving you, no matter what obstacle might try to get in the way. When you said yes, I baptized you in My love so that you would be able to savor its wonderful dimensions! My passion and tender lovingkindness for you is endless.

Here and now, your spirit is resting with Mine in My finished work. As you meditate on this eternal truth, you will begin to sense its reality in your soul. I can hardly wait for that breathtaking moment when you and I will see each other face to face!

Inspired by Psalm 23:2; 2 Timothy 3:16; 1 John 4:8, 16; 1 Corinthians 6:17; John 3:29; Jeremiah 31:3; John 3:16; Hebrews 12:2; Romans 5:5; 1 John 4:18;

Romans 8:37–39; 6:3–4; Ephesians 3:17–19; John 19:30; Hebrews 4:3; 1 Corinthians 13:12.

Day 17 – Do You Know Who You Already Are?

My flawless bride, more than anything, I long for you to know exactly who you *already* are in Me. This is vital because people act out of who they believe they are. It's likely that you view yourself in one of three different ways since you believed into Me.

One of the most common views is that you see yourself as *a sinner saved by grace*. You believe that you have been forgiven and that you are going to heaven when you pass from this earth, but you are still the same person you were before salvation. You believe that you have a sin nature at the core of your being and your desires and Mine are polar opposites most of the time.

Another commonly held view is that you believe you received a new nature in salvation, but your thoughts, feelings, attitudes, and actions indicate that the old you is still very much alive. Therefore, you see yourself as part good and part bad. *Part saint and part sinner.*

The only view that is filled with My truth and freedom is that you are *a saint who sometimes acts like a sinner.* Not only did you receive lifetime forgiveness and a new nature at salvation, but the bad old you—your sin nature—was crucified simultaneously with Me on the cross. You are now a brand-new creation because you were born again in Me when I was resurrected. You are in Me and I am in you forevermore! The desire of your new heart is not to sin, even though sometimes you still do because of the influence of this world, the flesh, and the devil.

Every day, you will prove your true identity either by sinning and being miserable or by happily expressing your true nature through dependence on My indwelling Spirit.

Inspired by Colossians 2:10; Proverbs 23:7; Hosea 4:6; John 8:32; Romans 1:7; 8:27; 1 Corinthians 1:2; 2 Corinthians 1:1; Ephesians 1:1; 2:19; Philippians 1:1; Colossians 1:2; 1 Thessalonians 3:13; Colossians 2:13–14; 2 Peter 1:4; Romans 6:6; Galatians 2:20; Colossians 3:3; 2 Corinthians 5:17; 1 Peter 1:3; John 14:20; 17:20–23; Ezekiel 36:26; Jeremiah 31:33; Philippians 2:13; Hebrews 8:10; Ephesians 2:2–3; 6:11; Galatians 5:16–17; Romans 6:21; Titus 2:11–12.

Day 18 – Walk This Way

My righteous bride, there are only two ways in which those who belong to Me can choose to walk in this world: in trusting dependence on My 24/7/365 indwelling Spirit or in reliance on the flesh. The flesh is not the old man (sin nature). Your sin nature, the "old you before Me," was crucified with Me on the cross. It is history.

Walking by the flesh is a way of living in this world that is rooted in the deception of Satan, the enemy of your heart. The deception that who you are was not changed at salvation and that you can get your needs met apart from Me. When you walk by the flesh, you are living just as if you are not one spirit with Me. The heart of all sin (walking according to the flesh) is the independent *I-can-do-it-myself* mindset.

It is impossible for you to walk by My Spirit and the flesh at the same time. Both ways of living are polar opposites. Walking by My Spirit is all about our union and your dependence on My power within you to carry out our common desire: *holiness*. That's right. Your heart's desires are in complete harmony with Mine. That happened the very moment you first believed into Me.

On the other hand, walking by the flesh is all about you forgetting our union and attempting to do life apart from My inspiration and empowerment. It takes time for you to develop the habit of relying on My supernatural resources instead of on your natural strength and abilities. From the time you were born, the ways of this world conditioned you for self-sufficient independence.

So, give yourself a break when you realize you are walking by the flesh rather than by My Spirit. Adjust your focus to walking in the truth of our eternal union, and you will experience happiness in the harmony of doing life together with Me.

Inspired by Galatians 5:13, 16, 25; Proverbs 3:5–6; Romans 6:6; Galatians 2:20; Colossians 3:3; Matthew 13:39; 1 Corinthians 6:17; John 14:20; 17:20–23; Galatians 5:17; Jeremiah 31:33; Philippians 2:13; 4:13; Hebrews 8:10; Romans 8:6; 2 John 1:4; 3 John 1:3–4.

Day 19 – The Most Beneficial Habit

My flawless bride, the most beneficial thing you can do upon waking each day is to *remember who you are*. To remind yourself of what is already true about your eternal spiritual union with Me. In other words, "do not be conformed to this world, but be transformed by the renewing of your mind."

Conform means to take an outward form that is inconsistent with who you really are on the inside. To act like someone you're not. The meaning of *transform* is the opposite of conform: to take an outward form consistent with who you really are on the inside. To simply be yourself. My desire is for your true (and only) self to be expressed.

One of the greatest obstacles to making your outside match your inside lies in the realm of your soul: feelings you experience that don't line up with your true identity. Continually allow My

Word and indwelling Spirit to drive your life rather than your feelings. Feelings are most often "thought responders," so if you want to change your feelings, you need to change what you are thinking about. The mind set on trusting dependence on My indwelling Spirit results in calm serenity and the vibrant expression of our holy union. On the contrary, when you are not relying on Me, you are automatically relying on the flesh. And reliance on the flesh is a dead end. A life-and-peace thief.

When your focus is not on My indwelling Spirit and your flawless identity in me, you will be controlled by your outward circumstances and feelings, conformed to this world. As a result, the expression of your true self is hindered.

On the other hand, when you focus on the truth of My indwelling Spirit and your pure, righteous, and holy identity in Me, the flow of My life in your spirit is released into your soul (conscious thoughts, feelings, attitudes) and body (actions). This is what it means to be filled with My Spirit. To be transformed by the renewing of your mind. *To be yourself.*

Inspired by Song of Songs 4:7; 6:9–10; 2 Corinthians 5:17, 21; Hebrews 10:14; 1 Corinthians 3:16–17; 6:17; Romans 12:2; Galatians 5:17, 19–21; 1 Thessalonians 5:19; Galatians 5:16, 18, 22–25; Ephesians 5:18.

Day 20 – When You Stumble in the Dance

My love, in this dance called "new life in Christ," you may be wondering what to do when you stumble, interrupting the flow of My grace. You were dancing so well, resting in My arms and enjoying My leading. What caused you to stumble?

I'll tell you. You were tripped up the moment you took your eyes off Me and put them on your feet, trying to make sure you were getting all the steps "right." Even though that seemed like the proper thing to do, it only made you to stumble more. And all of those missteps and mess ups ultimately caused you to stop enjoying your dance with Me. *This simply will not do!* This dance with you was the joy set before Me while I endured the cross.

My stunning bride, when (not *if*) you stumble in this dance, you have a choice to make. You can keep looking at your feet—wasting precious time—or you can put your attention squarely on

My loving gaze and allow Me once again to sweep you off your feet. Can you hear the background music? They are playing our song! It's called the "Song of the Lamb." The song of grace.

When you entrust yourself entirely to My leading, the gorgeous expression of our dance on this earth will be love, joy, peace, patience, kindness, goodness, faithfulness, gentleness, self-control, and righteousness. That's when you will once again enjoy wondrous delight in our dance. And that, My love, is the greatest desire of My heart!

Inspired by 1 Corinthians 5:17; Galatians 6:15; 5:7; Colossians 3:2; Hebrews 12:2; Philippians 4:8; Galatians 5:17; Proverbs 14:12; 16:25; 1 Timothy 6:17; James 3:2; Revelation 15:3; John 2:24; 1 Peter 2:23; Galatians 5:16, 22–25; Hebrews 12:11.

Day 21 – Where Your Joy and Peace Are Found

My dearest darling, it is necessary for Me to remind you of what is true again and again. You live and breathe in a world that continually broadcasts negative messages, trouble, and tragedy. To combat these potentially debilitating distractions, a continual focus on spiritual reality is what you need most.

The gospel—the best news you will ever hear, believe, and receive—is that I was crucified, buried, raised to new life, and seated at the right hand of My Father in heaven so that you could be united with Me in eternal bliss. While it is true that you won't experience uninterrupted joy and peace in your circumstances on this earth, you will experience both with Me throughout eternity! In the meantime, you will experience joy and peace to the degree that you set your mind on eternal reality. To the degree that you *believe Me*.

You have been completely forgiven for the sins of your entire lifetime—past, present, and future. I paid a horrific price so that the sin issue between you and Me could be obliterated forever. And you cashed in on this incredible gift when you believed into Me! The religious world will tell you, "Focus on your sins so you can overcome them." But I say, "Focus on Me and My finished work on the cross and experience wondrous delight!"

When you believed into Me, the old sin-loving you was crucified with Me on the cross and the new Son-loving you was born in My resurrection. The one and only flawless you is pure, righteous, and holy forevermore!

If you hope to find sustained joy and peace in the circumstances of this world, you will be disappointed, discouraged, and possibly even depressed. The only place you will consistently find true joy and peace is in believing Me.

Inspired by Song of Songs 4:7; Philippians 3:1; John 16:33; Hebrews 12:1–2; 2 Corinthians 4:17–18; Romans 1:16; 6:6; Galatians 2:20; Ephesians 2:4–6; Colossians 1:22; 2:12–13; 3:1–4; 1 Peter 1:3; 2:24; John 15:11; 16:24; 17:13; Romans 14:17; 15:13; Ephesians 1:7; 4:32; Colossians 1:13-14; 2:13-14; Hebrews 10:10, 14; John 3:16; 19:30; 2 Corinthians 5:17, 21; 1 Corinthians 3:16–17; Romans 8:6.

Day 22 – If You Are Doing This, You Are Not Loving

My treasure, the snares of the flesh can trip you up as you walk through this world. These traps are cleverly devised by the enemy of your heart. One of the most common and destructive snares is *judgment*—a negative focus on the visible flaws in your own and others' appearance and behavior.

Even though you may not realize it, you are doing math when you judge another person. You are taking away from their value in order to add to yours. You do this because you don't understand the *unsurpassable* value you already have. I long for you to believe the truth that you will never be worth more or less to Me than you are in this moment.

It is impossible to unconditionally love someone and judge them at the same time. Judgment and no-strings-attached love are mutually exclusive. And judging yourself is just as destructive as judging someone else. When you find yourself steeped in self-judgment and judging others, you need to come back to "God's Love 101" and meditate on truth. The truth of My limitless, unchanging love for you and the entire human race.

The ultimate worth of anything is determined by what the highest bidder is willing to pay in order to possess it. You, along with every other person who has ever existed, or will exist, have *unsurpassable worth*. This is because I paid the highest price—My life—so that you could become Mine forever by believing into Me.

Inspired by Galatians 5:13–14, 16–17; John 6:63; 1 Peter 5:8; John 7:24; 8:15; 12:47; 2 Corinthians 5:16; 1 Peter 4:8; Romans 8:6; 13:14; Titus 3:4–5; Jeremiah 31:3; John 3:16; Romans 5:8; 12:9–10; Ephesians 2:4–5; 3:15–19; 2 Timothy 1:7; 1 John 4:8, 16; 1 Peter 1:18; Ephesians 1:14; 1 Corinthians 6:20; 7:23.

Day 23 – You Were Made for This!

My beloved, I created you and every other human being with an intrinsic need to experience My unconditional love, value, and acceptance. I designed life in this world so that the only thing that will meet these needs perfectly is a dependent love relationship with Me.

Sadly, from the cradle to the coffin, from taking your first steps to your last breath, this fallen world's system conditions you to *earn* and *deserve* love, value, and acceptance through living on a performance-based treadmill. This may surprise you, but your hunger to experience no-strings-attached affection, worth, and belonging goes far beyond a humanistic need to feel good about yourself; it is implanted by Me and can only be satisfied by eternal spiritual union with Me.

When you look to sources outside of Me to meet these essential needs, you will end up disappointed. All of these self-sufficient habit patterns can be lumped into a single word: *flesh*. These patterns are stored in the memory banks of your brain and can appear attractive, average, or repulsive, depending on the eye of the beholder. Of course, all flesh patterns are repulsive to Me simply because they exclude Me from the equation. They find their source in *I've got this!* rather than reliant confidence in Me to meet every need.

It is important for you to realize, however, that I will never find *you* repulsive—regardless of the flesh patterns you may exhibit in your daily living. I perfectly separate your *true who* from your *do* and want you to realize that I define you by the flawless identity I gave you when you first believed into Me.

So rest easy. When you realize you are trying to experience fulfillment apart from Me, repent. Change your attitude from outsourcing to trusting dependence on My indwelling Spirit. You were made for this!

Inspired by Psalm 139:13–14; Romans 5:8; 1 John 4:8, 16; Ephesians 1:4–5; John 15:5; 1 Corinthians 6:17; John 14:20; 10:28; Hebrews 13:5; 2 Timothy 2:13; John 6:63; Romans 8:4–6; 13:14; Galatians 5:13, 16–17; Proverbs 3:5–6; Philippians 4:19; 2 Corinthians 5:16–21; Matthew 11:28–30; Hebrews 4:3.

Day 24 – Your Responsibility

My dearest darling, have you noticed that this fallen world is becoming more hostile as time goes by? And don't be fooled. It's not just unbelievers spewing their wrath. Believers walking by frustrated and angry flesh can be found on every street corner. The intensity of this type of flesh has grown to the degree that it is now called *rage*. Why are so many people, including My bride, expressing this type of repulsive behavior?

The last time you got frustrated and angry more than likely had to do with blocked goals. When you adopt goals outside of your control—like getting something or someone else to do what you want them to do—sooner or later you will find yourself gritting your teeth.

There's a much better (and more peaceful) way to navigate life in this world. Intentionally adopt goals within the realm of your control, according to My will, and in reliance on My indwelling

Spirit, and you will find yourself enjoying many more moments of your life.

As long as you live in this world, it is important for you to realize that your responses to your circumstances are *your* responsibility. I've given you the gift of choice. You are not a mindless drone that I control, but a holy heart whose deepest desires perfectly match Mine.

When you set your mind on negative circumstances beyond your control, you will react with anger and frustration. But when you set your mind on the truth of our eternal spiritual union and consistently enjoy intimacy with Me, you will experience and exude life and peace.

Inspired by Genesis 3; John 6:63; Galatians 5:20; Philippians 2:13; Proverbs 3:5–6; John 15:5; Galatians 5:16; Romans 15:18; 1 Timothy 6:17; Romans 6:11–13; Galatians 5:17; Ezekiel 36:26; Jeremiah 31:33; Hebrews 8:10; Romans 8:6.

Day 25 – The First Facet of Forgiving Others

My holy bride, one of the most damaging snares of the flesh is a refusal to forgive someone who has hurt you. Regardless of whether they wounded you on purpose or unknowingly, you make a choice soon after the injury occurs. You either decide to lock them up in an imagined debtor's prison until they apologize and/or you stop feeling hurt, or you choose to forgive them, releasing them from the debt they owe you.

If you do not choose to forgive your offender, it will ultimately manifest in anger, bitterness, and resentment. Drinking from this multilayered cup of flesh is like swallowing poison and expecting the one who wounded you to get sick. And as long as you justify your refusal to forgive them, you will be miserable.

The fundamental reason for your misery is that you were not re-created in Me, the ultimate Forgiver, to express unforgiveness, bitterness, and resentment. Because of your eternal spiritual union with me, you are "a forgiven forgiver at heart." And anytime you act like someone you are not, you will experience unrest in your soul (and body).

Realizing that your new heart's desire is to forgive those who hurt you is the first facet of forgiving others. *Expressing forgiveness is simply befitting for a new creation in Me.* Stay tuned to discover the final, and often most mysterious, facet of this liberating process.

Inspired by Romans 8:6; Galatians 5:13–26; Ephesians 4:26–27, 31–32; Colossians 3:8–14; Ephesians 1:7; Colossians 1:13–14; 2:13–14; John 1:29; Hebrews 9:22, 26, 28; 10:1–3, 11–14, 18; 1 Peter 3:18; 1 John 2:12; Ezekiel 36:26; 1 Corinthians 6:17; 2 Corinthians 5:17–21; Colossians 1:27.

Day 26 – The Final Facet of Forgiving Others

My lovely bride, realizing that you are a "forgiven forgiver at heart" is the first facet of forgiving others. You now understand that your deepest desire is not to withhold forgiveness from someone who has wounded you. *Forgiving others is an authentic expression of the new you in Me.* But this understanding alone does not make your forgiveness toward those who have hurt you complete.

Remember when I told you that you could do nothing apart from Me? While it is certainly true that you will never be apart from Me, you can live just as if you do not possess the same power that raised Me from the dead. When you choose to "do life" apart from reliance on My indwelling Spirit, you are carrying out the desires of the flesh. And when it comes to forgiving someone who has hurt you, unless you trust My perfect power through your inability to completely forgive, the process will remain unfinished. As a result, you will live in confusion and experience unrest in your soul (and body).

Is there someone you need to forgive? If so, agree with Me, saying out loud, "Lord, I want to forgive (name the offender) because I am a completely forgiven forgiver in You. Thank You for forgiving me with no strings attached! I confess that I cannot forgive (name the offender) from the flesh, so right now, by the power of your Spirit in and through me, I choose to forgive (name the offender) for (name the offense). Lord, thank You that Your power to forgive is fully expressed through my inability to forgive. When the enemy tries to convince me that I have not forgiven (name the offender), I will remind him that, not only have I forgiven (name the offender), but that the forgiveness was completed by Your power in and through me."

Sometimes the person you need to forgive most is yourself. If you are punishing yourself for things you have done wrong, then you are devaluing My precious blood that was poured out to pardon the sins of your lifetime. Go back through the above confession and replace (name the offender) with (myself). Now smile, take a deep breath, and relax in the freedom that comes from forgiving others and yourself.

Inspired by 2 Corinthians 5:17–21; Ephesians 4:31–32; John 15:5; Zechariah 4:6; Romans 8:11; Ephesians 1:19–20; 2 Corinthians 12:8–10; Romans 15:18; Matthew 26:26–28; Psalm 32:2; Romans 4:8.

Day 27 – Your Settled Significance in Christ

My dearest darling, though you may not realize it, it is possible that you are trying to find your significance in this world through your vocation. It doesn't matter whether you are the CEO of a Fortune 500 company, a schoolteacher, janitor, or stay-at-home mom. If you think your value and importance come from what you do, then a crucial question must be answered. What happens when you lose your job, you become medically disabled, your grown children leave, and so on? *Where,* then, do you find your sense of purpose and importance?

The only solid ground you can stand on in this life is realizing that your significance comes from Me alone. I created you and gave you unsurpassable worth by dying on the cross for you. I have never stopped loving you and never will, regardless of what you do or don't do. The very fact that you exist means that I wanted you. And you took My breath away when you said yes to eternal spiritual union with Me! That was the one "work" I required of you. *Belief into Me.*

You are (and always will be) as beautiful as the full moon and as pure as the sun. *Apart from what you do.* Yes, that's right. Absolutely gorgeous in Me! Stop wasting precious time in this world trying to make something of yourself when I have already made you perfect in Me. When you begin to realize My work in you is finished, you will begin to rest in your settled significance in Me.

Inspired by Galatians 3:27–38; 2 Corinthians 13:5; John 14:20; Psalm 139:13–16; John 3:16; Romans 5:8; 1 Peter 3:18; Jeremiah 31:3 Acts 17:24–31; 1 Corinthians 6:17; Ephesians 5:22–32; John 6:28–29; Song of Songs 6:10; 5:2; 6:9; John 19:30; Hebrews 10:10, 14; 4:3, 9–11.

Day 28 – The Gift of His Voice

My dearest darling, I am your life, the source of everything you need. My Spirit and your spirit are flawlessly fused together forever in your new heart—not in your head. If I asked you to close your eyes and point to yourself, you would point to your heart instead of your head. *Who you are is your new heart.*

Through the negative circumstances in your life, your head can get cluttered with noisy reasoning, confusion, assumptions, and speculations. When you are "in your head," unrest, stress, and a general sense of discontentment are the order of the day. There's a much better way to live: from your new heart, where you and I live together in perfect unity.

You can shut out disturbing distractions by redirecting your attention to the quiet stillness in your heart. This is where I am, continually speaking truth. I am the way, the truth, and the life. And I am always loving you perfectly. When you need to hear from Me, *get out of your head and into your heart*. I alone hold the answers to every question you have.

You can trust Me to cause you to hear My voice, whether you are sitting with your Bible open in the calm of the morning, or you are going through the ordinary activities of your daily life. I cherish our intimate times together when you acknowledge our union and are tuned into My voice. But if you're honest, you have to admit that a large part of your time on earth is spent focused on the task at hand rather than intently listening for My voice. I am not limited by your limitations. With Me, *nothing is impossible*. I can cause you to hear My voice whether you are listening or not.

I also speak to you through My written Word. While My entire Word was written for your knowledge, not all of it is written *to* those who are in Me. In fact, many of My very own words were spoken to those who were living under the Law in order to show them the futility of trying to keep it perfectly. My new covenant of grace did not come into effect until My death. When you read My words, it is essential that you remember the covenant under which they were spoken.

I speak to you through colorful, countless ways. Ways that include, but are not limited to: thoughts and impressions that agree with new covenant teaching, your new heart's desires, the circumstances of your life, and other people. Trust Me, dear one, to cause you to hear My voice at just the right time.

Inspired by Colossians 3:4; 1 Corinthians 6:17; Ezekiel 36:26; Psalm 46:10; John 14:6; 1 John 4:18; Jeremiah 33:3; Luke 1:37; 2 Timothy 3:16–17; Hebrews 8:13; 9:15–17; John 10:16, 27; 18:37.

Day 29 – He Is Not Convicting You

My beloved, after I absorbed the sin of the world, before I took My last breath, I cried out on the cross, "It is finished!" *Finished* means that I paid off your lifetime sin debt. And the moment you believed into Me, you cashed in on that precious payment. One of the most marvelous results of your belief and resulting union with Me is that I have declared you "not guilty" once, for all time and eternity.

I want to clear up something the church at large has believed for years because of a misrepresentation of My Word. One function of My Spirit is to "convict the world concerning sin and righteousness and judgment." When I *convict* someone, I am declaring them "guilty." Please notice that the object of My Spirit's conviction is *the world*. While it is true that you are in this world, you are not *of* this world. This means that you, dear one, are no longer a recipient of My Spirit's conviction.

This may cause you to wonder, *if it's not Your conviction that grabs my gut when I sin, then what is it?* I'll tell you. It is a godly sorrow that results when My Spirit testifies together with your spirit concerning behavior that does reflect your flawless identity in Me. A godly sorrow that lovingly motivates you to repent—change your mind—and express actions befitting for those who are Mine. You will always prove who you are through expressing righteousness (being yourself) and living fulfilled or sinning and being miserable.

Though My Spirit never convicts you or any other believer of sin, He faithfully operates in your life through loving you, strengthening you, comforting you, helping you, praying on your behalf, and guiding you into all truth.

Inspired by 2 Corinthians 5:21; John 19:30; Colossians 2:13–14; John 3:16; 1 Corinthians 6:17; John 14:20; John 16:8–10; 15:19; 17:16; 1 John 5:19; Romans 8:16; 2 Corinthians 7:9–10; Revelation 2:5; Galatians 5:16; Colossians 3:12–14; Titus 2:11–12; Romans 5:5; Philippians 4:13; Ephesians 3:16; Acts 9:31; John 14:26; 16:7; Romans 8:26; 16:3; 1 John 2:27.

Day 30 – How to Stop Sinning

My love, when you sin and I make you aware of it, there are generally two ways you will respond. The outcome of one is misery; the outcome of the other is happy holiness.

Let's start with the wrong way to respond. Because your thinking has not yet been fully renewed with truth, you feel dirty and distant from Me. And because emotions are powerful motivators, you mentally disconnect from Me, convincing yourself that I have left you. *After all,* you reason, *how could a perfect and holy God stand to be in the presence of one who has failed so miserably?* My Spirit is not the source of this reasoning.

The right way to respond to sin begins with acknowledging truth. The truth that your clean and close union with Me will never be altered by your behavior. The wonderful life-filled truth is that, when you sin, I am right there in your new heart doing what I do best—unconditionally loving you and motivating you to turn away from it. I never change, regardless of what you do or don't do. But if you believe the lie that I leave you or turn my heart away from you when you sin, by *whose power* will you be able to stop sinning?

When you fully consider the answer to this question, you will realize that it makes no sense at all for you to do anything but fix your eyes on My indwelling Spirit, thank Me for My power to turn from your sin, and get back to delightfully expressing your holy self in Me.

Inspired by Romans 14:23; 1 Corinthians 10:13; Romans 8:6; 12:1–2; 2 Corinthians 5:7; 10:5; John 14:20; 15:3; 1 Corinthians 3:16–17; 6:17; Ezekiel 36:26; Romans 5:5; Titus 2:11–12; Hebrews 13:8; James 1:17; 2 Corinthians 12:9–10; Hebrews 12:1–2; Galatians 5:16; Philippians 4:13.

Day 31 – His Prescription for Godly Feelings

My lovely bride, the feelings you experience are powerful motivators. So it is important to remind yourself of their proper place in your life. Feelings are in the realm of your soul and body. They are responders to whatever you are thinking about. If you meditate on what is true, godly feelings will accompany those thoughts. Conversely, if your focus is not on eternal spiritual reality, then ungodly feelings will naturally result as the negative circumstances of this world come at you.

Although feelings are great followers of realized truth, they are lousy leaders. *It is much easier to believe your way into a new way of feeling than to try to feel your way into a new way of believing.* Don't count on your feelings to convey truth, unless they are responding to beliefs concerning Me and your flawless identity in Me.

I want you to continually allow the truth—My Word and My indwelling Spirit—to take the driver's seat in your life rather than your feelings. If you are feeling lousy, then think about what you have been thinking about. I have entrusted you with the incredible privilege (and My power) to choose your thoughts. To experience godly feelings, simply replace your wrong thinking with what is true, good, and right. Think about things that are pure and lovely. Always think the best of people, instead of the worst. Think about everything you can praise Me for and be happy about. This is My tried-and-true prescription for godly feelings.

Inspired by 1 Thessalonians 5:23; Hebrews 4:12; Romans 8:6; Proverbs 4:20–22; John 14:6; 2 Corinthians 5:17; Song of Songs 4:7; Romans 12:2; 1 Corinthians 2:16; 2 Corinthians 10:5; Ephesians 4:22–23; Colossians 3:2; Isaiah 26:3; Philippians 4:8–9, 13.

Day 32 – Relaxed Reliance on Him

My treasure, the instant you believed into Me, My divine power deposited everything you need for life and godliness into your new heart. And now you have the choice to either rely on My limitless supply by faith or to exhibit a conscious (or subconscious) attitude of *I've got this, Lord. I'll let you know if I need your help.* When you do life with an independent mindset—as if you aren't in 24/7/365 union with Me—you are not walking in the truth, by My Spirit. And the worst part of it all is that you are missing out on the enjoyment that comes from conscious dependence on Me.

You might be wondering, *how can I know when I am walking by your Spirit?* It is simple. Walking by My Spirit is a posture of the soul. An attitude of relaxed reliance on Me. Each day upon waking, acknowledge My intimate partnership with you and ask

Me to live through you. Your part is to *trust Me to live My life through you*, and My part is to *live through you*.

This is walking by faith, not by sight or feelings. In the same way you trusted Me for your salvation, trust Me to live through you each day. Because this occurs in the spiritual realm, you are not necessarily going to feel My life coursing through your veins as you walk by faith. If you consistently felt My power through you, faith wouldn't be necessary.

Today, practice trusting Me to do all your tasks through you, even the seemingly insignificant ones like brushing your teeth and combing your hair. And then, do the same thing tomorrow. And the next day. This way, relaxed reliance on Me will become a restful, fruitful way of life for you.

Inspired by Deuteronomy 26:18; John 3:16; 2 Peter 1:3; 2 Corinthians 5:7; John 14:20; 1 Corinthians 16:7; 2 John 1:4; 3 John 1:3–4; Galatians 5:16; John 15:11; 16:24; 17:13; Romans 14:17; 15:13, 18; Galatians 2:20; 3:3; Colossians 2:6; Philippians 4:13; Hebrews 11:1, 6; Colossians 3:4; Hebrews 4:3, 11; Philippians 1:22.

Day 33 – He Died in Your Place

My joy, I long for you to understand the splendid significance of what I did on your behalf at the cross. I was pierced through for everything you've ever done and ever will do wrong. The sins of your lifetime were literally taken away from you (just as if you had never committed them) and transferred into My body (just as if *I* were the One who committed them). And then I allowed Myself to be punished—beaten, bruised, broken, and slaughtered—so that you could be forever made whole.

This may be difficult for you to comprehend, but *I loved you* even before you were born. Before one thought of Me entered your mind. Before you could do anything to merit My love. And I was right there loving you when you committed the worst, most shameful (in your mind) sin of your life. Yes, your sin was great, but My grace is greater than all your sin. I love you, no matter what you do or don't do. And there's nothing you can do about it. It is what it is. *I AM who I AM.* I am unconditional love, and nobody will ever love you like I love you. You are the love of My life!

Anticipating the joy of eternal union with you was how I endured the horrifying violence of the cross. I paid the ultimate price so that we could be joined together forever in love. And if I had to, I would go through it all over again to capture your heart. But I don't have to. Once was enough to secure our happily forever after!

Inspired by Isaiah 53:5; 1 Peter 2:24; 2 Corinthians 5:21; Jeremiah 1:5; Romans 5:8; John 3:16; Romans 5:20; Ephesians 2:8–9; Exodus 3:14; 1 John 4:8; Hebrews 12:2; 1 Corinthians 6:17; John 14:20; 17:20–26; 1 Corinthians 6:20; 7:23; Romans 6:10; Hebrews 7:27; 9:12; 10:10; 1 Peter 3:18.

Day 34 – You Died with Him

My dearest darling, when you believed into Me, you were joined to My life. My life is eternal life. I have always been and will always be. The instant you became a partaker in My divine nature, you gained a new spiritual past, present, and future. You gained *My* past, present, and future. This means that the old you was there in Me when I was crucified on the cross. *The old you was literally crucified with Me.*

The dead old you was there in Me when I was buried in the tomb. And the brand-new you was born again through My resurrection. Isn't that fantastic! The new you was there in Me when I walked out of that tomb. And the new you was there in Me forty days after My resurrection, when I was taken up into heaven in a cloud and seated at the right hand of My Father. Right now, you are literally seated with Me in heaven!

Your old self was crucified with Me so that you would be freed from sin. Your new self is dead to (separated from) sin's controlling power and alive to (joined together with) Me. This means that, before you were born again, you didn't have any choice but to sin. *Whatever is not from faith is sin.* Now that you are free to choose, you can walk by faith and not by sight.

Through My death, I made you completely compatible—holy, blameless, and beyond reproach—with Me. You were raised up with Me through faith and made alive together with Me. And now that you have been raised up with Me, keep seeking the things above, where I am, seated at the right hand of God. For the old you has died and the new you is hidden with Me in God. When I am revealed, you will also be revealed because you are *in Me* forevermore.

Inspired by John 3:16; 1 John 1:2; 5:11, 20; 2 Peter 1:4; Romans 6:6–7; 2 Corinthians 5:14; Galatians 2:20; Acts 1:9; Ephesians 1:20; Colossians 3:1; Hebrews 1:3; 8:1; 10:12; 12:2; Ephesians 2:4–6; Colossians 2:12–13; 1 Peter 1:3; 2:24; Romans 6:11, 13; 14:23; 2 Corinthians 5:7; Colossians 1:22; 3:1–4; Ephesians 1:13.

Day 35 – Divine Humility

My holy and beloved one, divine humility is an inherent characteristic of those who are one spirit with Me. I laid aside My Deity when I came to this earth in the form of a bond-servant, being made in the likeness of men. I humbled Myself by becoming obedient—to the point of death on a cross. Even though I was rich, I became poor for your sake so that you might become rich through My poverty.

Everything I did, I did because I love you. I did so that you could become a partaker in My divine nature. Through My grace, you humbled yourself when you believed into Me. You understood that you did not have the power to deliver yourself from this dark world. Instead of placing faith in your ability to save yourself, you placed your faith in Me.

The moment you believed into Me, you were clothed with Me. And My humility—along with compassion, kindness, gentleness, patience, forbearance, forgiveness, and love—is woven into the fabric of your new heart. My humility will find its fullest expression through your life as you recognize that you are already a humble new creation in Me and rely on My grace and power within you. To the world it will look like you regarding others as more important than yourself. To the world it will look like Me.

Inspired by 1 Corinthians 6:17; Philippians 2:5–8; 2 Corinthians 8:9; John 3:16; Romans 5:8; 2 Peter 1:4; Acts 18:27; Colossians 1:13; Galatians 2:16; 3:26; Philippians 3:9; Colossians 1:4; 2:5; Galatians 3:26–27; Colossians 3:12–14; 2 Corinthians 5:17; Ezekiel 36:26; Jeremiah 31:33; Philippians 2:13; Hebrews 8:10; Romans 12:1–2; 2 Corinthians 5:7; Galatians 5:16; Philippians 4:13; Romans 15:18; James 4:6; 1 Peter 5:5; Philippians 2:3; Romans 8:29.

Day 36 – Sweat or Sweet Refreshment?

My blameless one, there is a vast difference between the sweat that comes from trying to be good enough to earn right standing with Me and the sweet refreshment that results from trusting that you have already been made the "righteousness of God" through faith in Me.

If you are still trying to achieve a works-based righteousness, rather than resting in your faith-based righteousness, you are walking in delusion. I implore you to examine the truth that both ways of living are mutually exclusive. No one will ever be made right with God by doing what the Law commands. God's righteousness has been revealed apart from the Law. It is obtained through faith in Me. I am the end of the "law for righteousness" to everyone who believes in Me.

If you could have been made acceptable to Me through obeying the Law, then it was completely unnecessary for Me to die. *Think about that!* Whoever seeks to be righteous by following certain works of the Law actually falls under the curse of the Law. Everyone who doesn't live by and do *all* that is written in the Law is cursed. If a law had been given which was able to impart life, then righteousness would indeed have been based on law. If the first covenant had been faultless, there would have been no need for a second covenant to replace it. When I speak of the new covenant, it means that I have made the first one obsolete. It's out of date. *Expired.* Now, tell Me, what do you do with something that has expired? Something that has lost its effectiveness?

And might I remind you that the old covenant Law of Moses was given exclusively to the Israelites, not Gentiles? The only covenant I have ever offered to Gentiles is the new covenant—the covenant of righteousness based on faith in Me alone.

Whether you are a Jewish or Gentile believer is of no matter to Me. You are all one in My Spirit. The law of the Spirit of life in Me has set you all free from the law of sin and death. So don't "sweat" your new life in Me. Instead, enjoy the sweet refreshment that comes from resting in My finished work on the cross.

Inspired by Ephesians 1:4; 2 Corinthians 5:21; Romans 3:20–22; 10:4; Galatians 2:21; 3:10, 21; Hebrews 8:7, 13; 7:18–19; Leviticus 26:46; Psalm 147:19–20; Romans 2:14; Ephesians 2:11–12; Romans 10:6; Philippians 3:9; Galatians 3:28; Romans 8:2; 6:23; Hebrews 4:3, 10; John 19:30.

Day 37 – You Do Not Have to Die to Self or Sin

My lovely bride, it is vitally important that you understand who you are and what you want. Your new heart's desires are in holy harmony with My heart's desires. *You do not want to sin!* If you believe the subtle, destructive lie from the enemy that you want the opposite of what I want, you will live in confusion. And I am not the author of confusion.

Sometimes it takes a while for believers to be convinced of this foundational truth. But most, after peeling away layers of deeply rooted flesh patterns and meditating on the truth of their new identities, end up experiencing the liberating revelation that they don't want to sin. At all.

I am not suggesting that you will no longer be *influenced* to sin now that you live in union with Me. What I am saying is that when you do sin, it brings nothing but misery because you aren't walking in truth. I've said it before and I'll say it again: you will prove your true identity either by sinning and being miserable or by happily expressing your true nature through dependence on My indwelling Spirit.

A major misunderstanding has evolved from the biblical phrase "die to sin." The phrase I'm speaking of is "die to self." Although you will not find this phrase in the original Greek text, its use in Christendom is epidemic. On the surface, the phrase may seem harmless. But for a new creation in Christ, it presents a whopping problem. It causes the believer to falsely conclude, *If I'm supposed to die to self, then I must be a bad person.* You can only imagine how much confusion this false self-perception brings to a pure, righteous, and holy creation in Me!

I bore your sins in My body on the cross so that, when you believed into Me, you would die to sin and live to righteousness. This means that, at salvation, you were instantly separated from sin's controlling power and forever joined to My righteousness. So let this matter be settled in your mind once and for all: *you don't have to die to self or sin.* Live Me instead.

Inspired by Ezekiel 36:25–27; 1 Corinthians 3:16–17; 6:17; Jeremiah 31:33; Philippians 2:13; Galatians 5:17; Hebrews 8:10; John 8:44; 1 Corinthians 14:33; John 6:63; Romans 13:14; 2 Corinthians 5:16–17; Romans 12:2; 2 John 1:4; 3

John 1:3; Galatians 5:16; Ephesians 4:24; Colossians 3:10; 1 Peter 2:24; Hebrews 10:14; 2 Corinthians 5:21; Colossians 3:12; Ephesians 4:23: Philippians 1:21.

Day 38 – He Wants You to Enjoy Life

My beautiful bride, I want you to enjoy life. I mean, really enjoy it. I have richly supplied you with all things to enjoy. What's more, I want you to realize that *I am your life* and the source of your greatest enjoyment.

You will delight in Me to the degree that you see, by faith, My utter delight in you. My delight in you is not based on what you do or don't do. It will never change, no matter what. I delight in and celebrate you at all times—simply because you are Mine. You are the object of My extravagant affection, the regal recipient of My lavishing love, grace, and mercy. You take My breath away!

I am always available to you. But it is your choice whether or not you will allow yourself to find your greatest satisfaction in Me. In a world that continues to search for happiness and meaning apart from Me, a heart fully satisfied in Me brings Me great glory.

In the time you have left on this earth, learn how to master the art of taking great delight in Me through practicing My presence. This simply means that you acknowledge that I am always in you and for you, loving and rejoicing over you. It means that you are giving Me the precious gift of your attention in a world filled with distractions. And when your time on this earth comes to an end, you will be able to say that you truly enjoyed life—because you intimately savored Me.

Inspired by Song of Songs 4:7; 1 Timothy 6:17; Colossians 3:4; John 10:10; 14:6; 15:11; 17:13; Philippians 4:4; 2 Corinthians 5:7; Romans 6:14; James 1:17; Hebrews 13:8; Zephaniah 3:17; Ephesians 2:4, 7; 1 Peter 2:9; Song of Songs 4:9; Matthew 28:20; Romans 8:38–39; Hebrews 13:5; Psalm 37:4; 90:14; 145:16; Isaiah 58:11; Jeremiah 31:25; Ecclesiastes 3:11; 1 Corinthians 6:20; Psalm 16:11; Colossians 1:27; Romans 8:31; Colossians 3:1; Hebrews 12:1–2; 1 John 5:12; John 6:35, 48.

Day 39 – All Your Sins Are Gone Forever

My pure bride, renewing your mind with new covenant truth often involves as much unlearning as it does learning. There is a popular, yet detrimental, misconception that continues to undermine the rest, peace, and joy of many Christians. It is in how they view their sins.

In the Old Testament, the blood sacrifices offered by the Levitical priests year after year on the day of atonement could never completely *take away* their own and their people's sins. They merely *covered* them from year to year. There is a world of difference between both concepts.

Imagine that you are preparing to entertain important guests in your home this weekend. You spend the entire week having the white carpet in your living room cleaned and planning the meals you are going to serve. The weekend arrives and your doorbell rings. As you walk to the door with a glass of grape juice in your hand, you trip and accidentally spill it on your white carpet.

Oh no! You don't want your company to see the mess you've made, so you go into another room and get a large area rug to cover up the stain until they leave. *Whew!* You breathe a sigh of relief that it is now out of sight. But it is definitely not out of your mind. You are very aware of the mess you are going to have to deal with after your guests are gone.

Although the sins of the Hebrew people were covered by blood sacrifices year after year, their relief was only temporary. They would be back in Jerusalem at the same time next year to get their sins covered once again.

You can rejoice in the truth that you don't live under the old covenant! You live under the new covenant where My one-time sacrifice made you perfect and clean forever the moment you believed into Me! I didn't just clean up your mess. I ripped out the old stained carpet, threw it away, and replaced it with brand-new, snow-white, stain-repelling carpet.

Rejoice in the truth that you never have to worry about the stain of unforgiven sin in your life. I have taken your sins away and perfected you for all time! If you will own this truth, you will experience delightful rest in knowing that *all your sins are gone forever!*

Inspired by Song of Songs 6:9–10; Luke 22:20; Romans 12:2; Song 2:15; 2 Corinthians 10:5; Hebrews 4:3, 9–10; Romans 14:17; Leviticus 23:27–28; Hebrews 10:1–4; 8:8, 13; 9:15; 12:24; 10:10–14; Ezekiel 36:25–27; 1 Corinthians 13:6; John 1:29; Hebrews 9:26; 1 John 3:5; Hebrews 4:2.

Day 40 – The Truth about Abiding

My beloved bride, the word *abide* is one that is often misunderstood in Christendom. The incorrect context in which believers use this word is that *abiding in Me* is something they are choosing to do or not do at any given moment. This can shift your attention from the rest and enjoyment that come from trusting that My work on the cross is finished to a hyper-introspection that breeds a debilitating "not enough" mentality. And you know exactly what that kind of thinking leads to!

You will experience great rest when you realize the truth about abiding. Abiding in Me is not something that you have to consciously remember to do! *Abiding in Me* simply means that you are "living in Me continually." It is an eternal state of being that I caused the moment you believed into Me.

Before the new covenant became effective through My death and resurrection, My Spirit did not abide in My people. Instead, I would come upon them at specific times to enable them to accomplish My purposes. But *now,* I live in you and you live in Me forever!

If you are still not convinced that abiding is referring to our eternal spiritual union, all you have to do is read My apostle John's first letter where he writes, "By this we know that we abide in Him and He in us, because He has given us of His Spirit." The meaning of abide is crystal clear. All believers in Me possess My Spirit, so they abide in me and I abide in them. Abiding in Me is a never-ending state for the believer in Christ.

In the same way that intimate union between a husband and wife can lead to the birth of children, a wonderful natural result of Me abiding in you and you abiding in Me is that you will bear much spiritual fruit—love, joy, peace, patience, kindness, goodness, faithfulness, gentleness, self-control, righteousness, truth, thankfulness, and praise.

Inspired by Song of Songs 6:3; John 19:30; Romans 8:6; John 3:16, 18; 6:40; Romans 4:5; John 15:4–7; Luke 22:20; Judges 3:10; 6:34; 14:6; 1 Samuel 10:9-10; John 14:17, 20; 17:21, 23; 1 Corinthians 3:16; 6:17, 19; 1 John 4:13; John

15:8, 16; Romans 7:4; Galatians 5:22–23; Ephesians 5:9; Philippians 1:11; Hebrews 12:11; 13:15.

Day 41 – Savoring the Reality of Your Union with Christ

My dearest darling, there are two aspects to your eternal spiritual union with Me: the invisible reality that is imperceptible to your natural senses and the experiential reality that is discernible to you—also known as communion. Simply put, *communion* is the awareness and enjoyment of your spiritual *union* with Me.

In order to savor the reality of our oneness, you need to acknowledge it and grow in your awareness of My powerful, loving presence in you at all times. You need to taste and see that I am good! No one in this world will ever love you like I love you because My love is not of this world. I always, always have your best interests at heart. My lovingkindness toward you will last forever.

Actual experience of My love for you is the springboard of true joy in your life. To have only a cognitive knowledge of My love for you without personally experiencing it would be like holding a plate of your favorite dessert in your hands without breathing in its rich aroma and enjoying every delectable morsel.

Once you taste sweet communion with Me, you'll come back for seconds, thirds, fourths, and … well, you get the point. And you will never gain a pound. Instead, the weight of burdens will melt away as you let Me shower you with My extravagant affection. And you won't be able to help but love Me back!

Inspired by 1 Corinthians 3:16; 6:17; John 14:20; 1 John 4:13; Philemon 6; Romans 8:6; 12:2; 2 Timothy 1:7; Ephesians 2:4; 3:16–20; Psalm 34:8; Jeremiah 31:3; Psalm 100:5; 106:1; Romans 5:5; 1 Corinthians 13:4–8; Galatians 5:22; 1 John 4:8, 16, 19.

Day 42 – Let Him Love You

Love of My life, there is nothing you could do to cause me to love you more than I already do. And there is nothing you could do to cause me to love you less. My love for you does not fluctuate based on your behavior. Rather, it has everything to do with Who I am. And I am perfect love.

What's more, My love for you is not a generic, one-size-fits-all love. It is private and personal. *Exclusive.* It is a love that knows you inside and out. A love that knows all your favorite things. Your favorite food. Your favorite love song. Your favorite season. Your favorite sport. Your favorite book. Your favorite movie.

I know what moves your heart, your deepest struggles, and every dark thought you have ever entertained. I know every unkind word from your mouth and everything about your attitudes and actions that you detest. Yet My love for you is a love that completely separates your behavior from your identity and looks straight into your heart, proclaiming, "You are lovely and pure, and I want you to know and believe the love I have for you."

My love is a love that will never leave you. It is a love that says, "I will be your everything in all circumstances. Just *let* Me. Let Me love you out of the fear you are feeling. Let Me love you out of the mess you are dealing with. Let me love you out of the sin you are struggling with. Let me love you out of the addiction that you have been trying to get free from." When you let Me love you in the midst of your weakness, you are allowing My love to find its fullest expression!

Inspired by 1 John 4:8, 16, 18; Psalm 139:1–18; Song 1:5, 10; 2:14; 4:3; 6:4, 9–10; Deuteronomy 31:6; Hebrews 13:5; Romans 8:35–39; 2 Corinthians 12:9–11; John 3:16; Romans 5:5, 8; Ephesians 2:4; 3:19; Titus 3:4; 1 John 4:9–10; Jude 1:21.

Day 43 – Peace in His Sovereign Care

My treasure, everything I do and allow in your life finds its source in My sovereign love and care for you. *I am in control.* You can rest in knowing that—even though there are times in your life when it looks like everything is out of control—nothing escapes My superintending guidance. I have established My throne in the heavens, and My sovereignty rules over all. I do whatever I please. No one can ward off My hand or question My actions.

You will experience a peace that surpasses all human comprehension when you realize that neither the most minuscule details of your life nor its most pressing issues escape My loving attention. If I am sovereign over all of my creation, then don't you think that I am well able to manage every aspect of your life in My perfect timing?

In order for you to experience My peace in this world, you will need to relinquish the fleshly desire to have everything figured out. The mind of man plans his way, but I direct his steps. I alone hold all the answers to your most troubling questions. And if I want you to know something, I will reveal it to you. The peace you experience in this world is not found in Me giving you all the answers to your every question. It will flow like a gentle river through your soul when you are resting in the truth that I am working all things together for your good, no matter what.

Inspired by Psalm 103:19; 115:3; Daniel 4:35; Philippians 4:7; Psalm 139:1–18; Ephesians 3:9; Revelation 4:11; Psalm 31:15; Ecclesiastes 3:1, 11; Acts 1:7; Galatians 4:4; 2 Peter 3:8; 1 Timothy 6:15; John 14:1, 27; Proverbs 3:5–6; 16:9; Psalm 147:5; 1 John 3:20; Isaiah 40:28; Jeremiah 29:11–13; 33:3; Isaiah 66:12; Romans 8:28.

Day 44 – The Truth about Healing

My dearest darling, if you are hurting, either emotionally or physically (or both), I want you to understand that *I, the Lord, am your healer.* I heal your broken heart and bandage your wounds. I am full of compassion for you in your suffering. *I hurt when you hurt.* I bore your sins in My body on the cross so that you would be healed by My wounds.

Your spirit (who you are now and forever) has already been made whole through your union with Me. There is *nothing* lacking in you. You have eternal life and that includes a new resurrection body like Mine. A body not stained with sin. A God-infused body that you will get to enjoy for all eternity. Isn't that marvelous!

Your guaranteed healing will not always include a manifestation of emotional and physical health in the here and now. If you have asked Me to heal your damaged emotions and/or your physical maladies, I want to encourage you. I want to assure you that there is nothing wrong with you or your faith. Through our union, you possess My faith—the very same faith I exercised while I walked this earth! Yes, I had to completely depend on My Father to live His life through Me over two thousand years ago. And now you get to choose whether or not you will depend on My life in and through you during your brief stay here.

If you have contributed to your suffering through poor choices, then I want you to partner together with Me so that you might enjoy a greater quality of life on this earth. I am your wisdom and I will lead and empower you to make healthy choices that can improve your well-being in the here and now.

Do I still perform miraculous healing on this earth? *Yes!* Do I want you to ask Me to manifest your emotional and physical healing in the here and now? *You bet I do!* And when you have asked, I want you to rest in the outcome, whatever it may be. I will never leave you nor stop loving you.

Inspired by Exodus 15:26; Psalm 103:2–4; 147:3; James 5:11; Isaiah 53:5; 1 Peter 2:24; Ephesians 1:3; Colossians 2:10; 2 Peter 1:3; 1 Corinthians 3:16; 6:17; John 14:20; 3:15–16, 36; 5:24; 6:40, 47; 10:28; 17:3; Romans 5:21; 6:22–23; Galatians 6:8; 1 Timothy 1:16; Titus 1:2; 3:7; 1 John 1:2; 2:25; 5:11, 13, 20; Daniel 12:2; John 6:44, 54; 11:24–25; Romans 6:5; 8:11; 1 Corinthians 15:21–

23, 35–55; 2 Corinthians 4:14; Philippians 3:10–11; Romans 6:6, 13; 7:23; 8:10; Revelation 21:4; Galatians 2:16, 20; 5:22; John 14:8–10, 24; 5:19, 30; 7:16; 8:28, 42; 12:49; Galatians 5:16; 1 Corinthians 7:35; 10:31; Philippians 4:8; Romans 6:21–22; 1 Corinthians 1:30; Acts 4:16, 22; Jeremiah 17:14; Hebrews 13:5; Jeremiah 31:3.

Day 45 – Where Thoughts Come From

My lovely one, it is important for you to understand *where* the thoughts you experience come from. They either originate with *you* or *outside of you*. Let's start with the thoughts that originate with you. There is a common misconception that man's thoughts are generated in the brain, but My Word describes them as being formed in the heart. You are a brand-new heart—a new spirit united in holy union with My Spirit. My Spirit is the Spirit of truth. Therefore, thoughts that issue from you will always reflect the righteousness and holiness that comes from truth.

Thoughts that originate outside of you are coming from the flesh or the environment in which you live. The *flesh* comprises the habit patterns stored in your physical brain that are rooted in Satan's deception and interfere with your dependence on My indwelling Spirit. Clearly, thoughts that issue from the flesh will always reflect the unrighteousness and unholiness that comes from lies. Satan is the father of all lies.

Information (in the form of thoughts) from your environment enters your brain through your physical senses of sight, hearing, taste, smell, and touch. These thoughts will reflect either truth or lies, depending on their original source. This is where your discernment and choice come in. I am your wisdom and I have entrusted you with the incredible ability to choose which thoughts you will accept (own and believe) and which thoughts you will reject (disown and disbelieve).

Your ability to choose is the most powerful gift I have given you. When you reject the truth and accept the lies, you will experience discontentment, forfeiting your enjoyment of life and peace on this earth. However, when you accept the truth and reject the lies, you will experience the refreshing transformation that comes from the renewing of your mind. You will enjoy the happy harmony that comes from walking in the truth, by My Spirit.

Inspired by Matthew 15:19; Mark 7:21; Luke 1:51; Hebrews 4:12; Ezekiel 36:26; 2 Corinthians 5:17; Ephesians 4:24; 1 Corinthians 3:16–17; 6:17; John 14:6, 17; 15:26; 16:13; 17:17, 19; Ephesians 4:24; John 6:63; Revelation 12:9; Galatians 5:16–17; John 8:44; Hebrews 5:14; Deuteronomy 30:19–20; Joshua

24:15; 1 Corinthians 1:24, 30; James 1:17; Song of Songs 2:15; Romans 12:2; 2 Corinthians 3:18; 10:3–5; Romans 8:6; 2 John 1:4; 3 John 1:3–4; Galatians 5:25.

Day 46 – What to Do with Rogue Thoughts

My cherished one, every day there is a battle going on in your mind. Your role in this battle is to accept (own and believe) thoughts based in truth and to reject (disown and disbelieve) thoughts based in lies. You will enjoy great rest and peace as you reject the lies. On the contrary, your days will be filled with unrest and distress when you do not reject the lies. These lies are like little foxes that—though they may seem small—end up destroying entire vineyards when allowed to run wild. I want you to catch the foxes that are keeping you from bearing the fruit of love, joy, peace, patience, kindness, goodness, faithfulness, gentleness, self-control, and righteousness.

Even though you walk in the flesh, you do not fight this battle according to the flesh. Your struggle is against spiritual forces of wickedness, not flesh and blood. I have given you a spiritual arsenal of truth, righteousness, peace, faith, salvation, and prayer to stand against Satan's schemes. These weapons contain My power to destroy speculations and every lofty thing that contradicts Me. Your responsibility is to wield these weapons, taking every rogue thought captive to My obedience.

What does it mean to take rogue thoughts captive to My obedience? My obedience was humbling Myself to the point of death on the cross. Through Adam's disobedience, everyone born into this world is a sinner. But through My obedience, all who believe in (*into*) Me are made righteous through their co-crucifixion and co-resurrection with Me. And because you are the righteousness of God in Me, *you cannot generate unrighteous thoughts.* To take every thought captive to My obedience, then, means that you judge the thoughts you experience in light of the truth of your righteous identity.

As you become accustomed to the knowledge of your righteousness, through practice, you will train your senses to discern good (righteousness) and evil (unrighteousness). Now, when you become aware of an unrighteous thought, take it captive by saying out loud, "That thought did not come from me! I refuse to own, meditate, or act on it! I am the righteousness of God in Jesus Christ!"

Inspired by Romans 16:19; Hebrews 4:3, 11; John 14:27; Romans 8:6; 14:17; Song of Songs 2:15; Galatians 5:22–23; Ephesians 5:9; Philippians 1:11; Colossians 1:6, 10; Hebrews 12:11; James 3:18; 2 Corinthians 10:3–5; Ephesians 6:10–18; Philippians 2:8; Romans 5:19; John 3:16; Romans 6:6; Galatians 2:20; Colossians 3:3; 2 Corinthians 5:17, 21; Hebrews 5:13–14.

Day 47 – You Are a Victor, Not a Victim

My beloved, you are beginning to enjoy the freedom that comes from understanding that the unrighteous, unholy thoughts (lies) you hear in your mind do not originate with you, but with Satan, the father of all lies. Every untruth, every deception, ultimately finds its genesis in him.

Although Satan has absolutely no access to you (you are safely sealed in Me forever), I have given him limited access to your thought life. And if you are ignorant of his schemes, he can wreak havoc in your mind, influencing you to feel like a victim of the thoughts you experience. Your sole responsibility is to take every rogue thought captive, but that doesn't mean it is always easy to do. Your enemy is cunning.

The fact that you cannot see Satan inject the unrighteous, unholy thoughts gives him an advantage. And when you accept (own and believe) these rogue thoughts, you will experience the unrighteous, unholy feelings that accompany them.

Feelings, whether good or bad, are strong motivators. The way you think influences the way you feel, and the way you feel influences the way you act. It all starts with thoughts. If you have been feeling and acting in ways contrary to your pure, righteous, and holy identity in Me, then that means you have failed to capture the rogue thoughts (lies) provoking this unrighteous, unholy cycle of behavior.

If you want to enjoy the peaceful state of mind that I designed you to experience, you have to take control of your thought life by rejecting the lies you are believing and replacing them with My truth. You are not a powerless victim of the lies injected by Satan. Instead, you are a powerful victor through My Spirit of truth who indwells you. Now believe Me and act like the victor you already are!

Inspired by Galatians 5:1; John 8:44; Revelation 12:9; 2 Corinthians 1:22; Ephesians 1:13; 4:30; Luke 22:31; 2 Corinthians 2:11; Song of Songs 2:15; 2 Corinthians 10:3–5; Ephesians 6:10–18; Genesis 3:1–5; John 10:10; 2 Corinthians 11:3, 14; 1 Peter 5:8; Psalm 29:11; Isaiah 26:3; 55:12; John 14:27; 16:33; Romans 8:6; 14:17–19; 15:13; 1 Corinthians 14:33; Philippians 4:7; Colossians 3:15; 2 Thessalonians 3:16; Romans 12:2; 1 Corinthians 2:16;

Philippians 4:8; Hebrews 10:16; 1 John 3:19; Luke 4:1–13; James 4:7; 1 Peter 5:9; 1 Corinthians 15:57; 1 John 5:4.

Day 48 – Your Enemy's Most Effective Strategy

My lovely bride, although Satan cannot touch you spiritually, he can greatly hinder your experience and expression of My cherishing love and exuberant life. That is, *if you let him*. The only real power he has over you is when he can get you to believe his lies. Deceiver is his name; deception is his game. And if he can hoodwink you into owning the unrighteous thoughts he serves up to you, then he can control you.

Satan's most effective strategy is to disguise his thoughts as your own in order to trap you into doing his will. If you allow these insidious impostors to set up camp in your mind, they can do untold amounts of damage in your life. So, how exactly does Satan dress up his sinister suggestions to trick you into believing that you generated them? He feeds them to you in *first-person singular* pronouns (I, me, my, myself, etc.)! Can you see how thoughts like *I am such a loser! God doesn't really love me, My past will always come back to haunt me,* and *If this is going to get done right, I'm going to have to do it myself!* could easily cause you to conclude that they came from you?

If you could actually see that Satan was the source of these thoughts, you wouldn't even give them the time of day. But when you believe they originated with you, you will have a difficult time agreeing with Me that you are pure, righteous, and holy! And your spoken words and actions will ultimately reflect what you believe. In short, you will become a pawn in your enemy's hands when you take his bait.

Knowledge of your enemy's most effective strategy will motivate and empower you to take control of the atmosphere of your mind. So, the next time you hear a rogue thought in first-person singular, refuse to accept it and replace it with the truth about you. The wonderful, beautiful, flawless, eternal truth about you.

Inspired by 2 Corinthians 1:22; Ephesians 1:13; 4:30; John 8:44; Revelation 12:9; 2 Timothy 2:26; Song of Songs 4:7; 6:9–10; 1 Corinthians 2:16; 3:16–17; 6:17; 2 Corinthians 5:17, 21; Hebrews 10:10, 14; Song of Songs 2:15; 2 Corinthians 3:18; 10:3–5; Romans 12:2; Luke 4:1–13; James 4:7; 1 Peter 5:9; Revelation 19:7–9; 21:2.

Day 49 – Living in Love with Christ

My flawless bride, now that you have knowledge of your enemy's schemes, you will experience and express My cherishing love and exuberant life much more often. I didn't tell you that truth alone will set you free; I told you that *knowing* truth would cause you to experience the freedom I died to give you.

As long as you live on this earth, it will be your responsibility to take rogue thoughts captive. And I have given you everything you need to do this. I will never leave you alone in this battle. You can do all things through My strength!

While capturing rogue thoughts is a necessary defensive strategy in the battle going on in your mind, your best defense will always be a good offense. And one of the most effective ways you can be proactive is to allow Me to captivate your mind to the point that there is room for little else. I want you to think about everything that is true, honorable, right, pure, lovely, reputable, excellent, and praiseworthy. In doing so, you will be thinking about Me and all the good things that come from Me. When you become obsessed with Me, the things that don't matter *won't* matter.

I want you to keep your mind set on our eternal spiritual union. Right now, you are seated with Me in heaven. And at the same time, I am living within you on this earth, loving you perfectly. I want you to intentionally acknowledge and enjoy My personal affection for you. Let Me continually lavish you with My unconditional love, and you will find yourself falling more in love with Me every day!

Living in love with Me on this earth will cause you to see Me in everything. I will take your breath away with the sunrises and sunsets I paint for you to enjoy in just that moment in time. I will serenade you with love songs that will cause you to swoon over Me. I will reveal My love for you in countless ways each day as you keep your focus on Me. Living in love with Me on this earth is only way to truly live!

Inspired Song of Songs 4:7; Hebrews 10:10, 14; John 8:32; Song of Songs 2:15; 2 Corinthians 10:3–5; 2 Peter 1:3; Deuteronomy 31:6; Matthew 28:20; Hebrews 13:5; Philippians 4:13; Philippians 4:8; Hebrews 12:2; James 1:17;

Colossians 3:1–2; Ezekiel 36:27; John 14:20; 1 Corinthians 3:16; 6:17; Ephesians 2:6; 1 John 4:18; Jude 1:21.

Day 50 – Your Happily Forever After

My dearest darling, your *Happily Forever After* is a sure thing because of My finished work on the cross and your belief into Me. You are Mine and I am yours for all eternity. While it is true that you will not experience unending bliss while you live on this earth, you are guaranteed eternal happiness on a new earth because of your spiritual union with Me. Righteousness, peace, and joy will be the very air that you breathe in your glorified body as you walk hand in hand with Me in this never-ending wonderland.

You may be thinking, *this sounds too good to be true*, but I promised new heavens and a new earth to all who believe into Me. And I keep all of My promises! Even though your eyes have never seen and your ears have never heard and your heart has never fully contemplated what I have prepared for you beyond this life, I want you to spend time imagining it! Ask Me to inspire your imagination when you think about eternity.

The most majestic places on this earth, the most mesmerizing music, the most tantalizing aromas, the most delectable food, and the most sublime textures that you could experience on this earth pale by far in comparison to the sights, sounds, smells, tastes, and textures that you and I will enjoy together in eternity! And the best part of all? The most divine, sweet, and loving fellowship with Me and all the saints throughout the ages. So, tell everyone you know about the incredible hope you have in Me and invite them to their own *Happily Forever After!*

Inspired by John 19:30; 3:16; Song of Songs 2:16; 6:3; 7:10; 2 Peter 3:18; John 16:33; Isaiah 65:17; 66:22; 2 Peter 3:13; Revelation 21:1; Isaiah 52:7; John 14:20; 1 Corinthians 3:16; 6:17; Romans 14:17; 1 Corinthians 15:35–58; 2 Corinthians 1:20; 2 Peter 1:4; 1 Corinthians 2:9; Ephesians 3:20; Colossians 3:2; Acts 2:42; 1 Corinthians 1:9; 2 Corinthians 13:14; Philippians 2:1–2; Philemon 1:5–7; 1 John 1:3; Romans 8:24–25; 15:13; 2 Corinthians 3:12; Colossians 1:5; Titus 1:2; 1 Peter 1:3, 13; 3:15.

Kim K. Francis is the author of *His Banner over Me Is Pursuing Love: An Intimate, Interactive Study of the Song of Solomon, Chapters 1 and 2.* She delights in sharing the good news of the gospel of grace weekly on her blog, *A Happy Christian's Secret Life,* at www.kimkfrancis.com. She and her husband, Steven, reside in Perryton, Texas, and are the founders of His Heart's Desire Ministries, a ministry that helps believers around the world live loved in Christ through understanding their flawless identity in Him. Connect with Kim on Facebook, Twitter, and Instagram.

Made in the USA
Coppell, TX
01 December 2019

12171211R10085